Historical Ice-Out Dates for 29 Lakes in New England, 1807–2008

Open-File Report 2010–1214

U.S. Department of the Interior
U.S. Geological Survey

Cover. Photograph shows ice-out on Jordan Bay, Sebago Lake, Maine, Spring 1985.

Historical Ice-Out Dates for 29 Lakes in New England, 1807–2008

By Glenn A. Hodgkins

Open-File Report 2010–1214

U.S. Department of the Interior
U.S. Geological Survey

Contents

Figures

Tables

Historical Ice-Out Dates for 29 Lakes in New England, 1807–2008

By Glenn A. Hodgkins

Abstract

Ice-out dates for lakes are an important hydrologic data series for climate-change research. Historical ice-out dates for 29 lakes in New England from 1807 through 2008 were compiled and are presented in this report. Five lakes have more than 160 years of data and another 14 have more than 100 years of data. The oldest recorded ice-out date is for Sebago Lake in 1807.

Introduction

A *lake ice-out date* refers to the date in spring when the annual winter ice cover disappears from a lake. In mid-latitude areas of the northern hemisphere such as New England, ice-out dates can serve as useful indicators of late winter and early spring climate change. Lake ice-out dates have been historically recorded in New England for practical reasons, such as for lake transportation, and out of general interest.

Hodgkins and James (2002) compiled long-term ice-out data through 2000 for 29 lakes in New England from individuals, water companies, newspapers, State fish and wildlife agencies, power companies, and others. The current report updates the lake ice-out dates through 2008. This report would not have been possible without the collection, compilation, and archiving of lake ice-out dates by many people over the past two centuries, especially Charles B. Fobes of Portland, Maine. Mr. Fobes' interest in lake ice-out dates extended back to the 1940s (Fobes, 1945); he recorded dates from observers at many lakes in Maine over the years and compiled older historical data at lakes. Much of the data presented in this report would have been lost or never collected without Mr. Fobes' work. Some 63 known individuals and organizations, and several unknown sources, contributed the data presented in this report.

Compilation of Lake Ice-Out Dates

Records from all six New England states (Connecticut, Maine, Massachusetts, New Hampshire, Rhode Island, and Vermont) were searched for long-term lake ice-out dates. This was done primarily by calling town officials, lake associations, newspapers, and fisheries agencies, and following up on leads. It was not possible to search for records on all lakes. Particular attention was given to large lakes and lakes near towns. Long-term lake ice-out dates were found for 29 lakes in New England (fig. 1). Most of these lakes are in Maine, with a few in New Hampshire and Massachusetts. No long-term records were found for lakes in Vermont, Connecticut, or Rhode Island. Five lakes had more than 160 years of data and another 14 had more than 100 years of data. The oldest recorded ice-out date is for Sebago Lake in 1807.

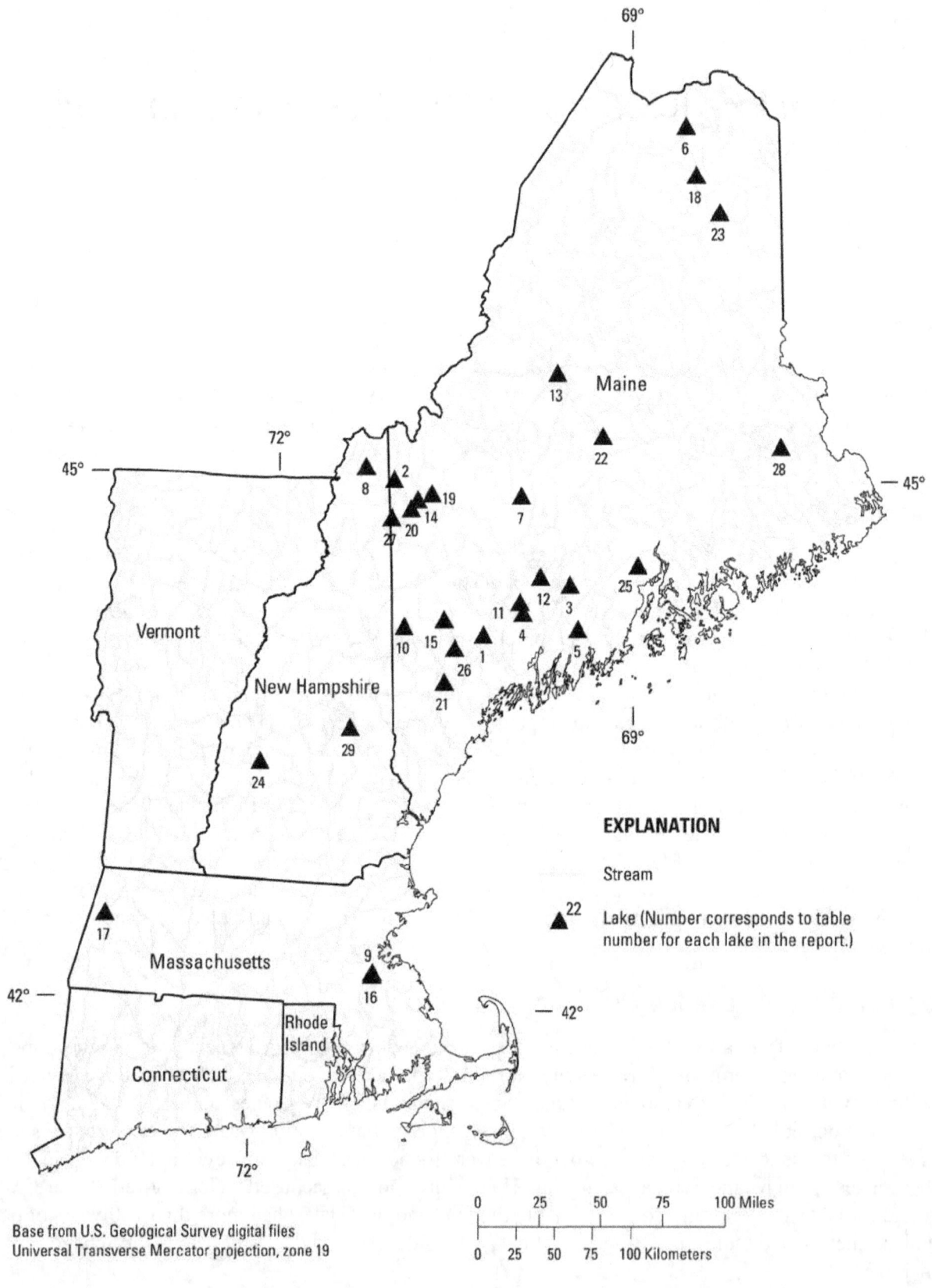

Ice-out definitions for individual lakes can vary over time and between observers. The exact definition (including the observation location) is not known with confidence in most cases. For lakes with overlapping data from more than one independent observer, the data that were judged to be most consistent over time with data from earlier and later time periods for that lake were used. No ice-out dates were estimated for years with missing data, and no adjustments to lake-ice observations were made, with the following exceptions: (1) 19 years of data at Damariscotta Lake and 2 years at Cobbosseecontee Lake were filled in from a secondary observer and adjusted by the average difference in the dates between the primary and secondary observers; (2) 1 year of data was excluded from the dataset for China, Damariscotta, Portage, and Sebec Lakes and 2 years were excluded for Messalonskee Lake because comparisons with other lakes in New England indicated these data were not reliable.

Lake ice-out dates in Julian days (January 1 of each calendar year is Julian day 1, January 2 is Julian day 2, and so forth) and observer names are given in tables 1 to 29. The latitude and longitude given in the tables are intended for general lake location only and do not necessarily represent the ice-out observation location. The geographic locations of the 29 lakes are shown in figure 1, and the numbers in figure 1 correspond to the table numbers for each lake.

References Cited

Fobes, C.B., 1945, The ice clearing dates of the Maine Lakes: Bulletin of the American Meteorological Society, v. 26, no. 8, p. 331–333.

Hodgkins, G.A., and James, I.C. II, 2002, Historical ice-out dates for 29 lakes in New England: U.S. Geological Survey Open-File Report 02–34, 32 p.

Table 1. Ice-out dates for Lake Auburn, Maine.

[--, no data]

Location of lake—Latitude 44°08'40", longitude 70°15'00"

Period of record—1836 to 2008

Years of record—166

Observers—Auburn Water District, Union Water Power Company, FPL Energy Maine, Lewiston Sun-Journal

Year	Julian day	Year	Julian day	Year	Julian day	Year	Julian day	Year	Julian day
1807	--	1848	108	1889	107	1930	104	1971	121
1808	--	1849	104	1890	116	1931	101	1972	127
1809	--	1850	121	1891	117	1932	111	1973	107
1810	--	1851	111	1892	112	1933	112	1974	100
1811	--	1852	128	1893	125	1934	113	1975	119
1812	--	1853	112	1894	114	1935	115	1976	108
1813	--	1854	126	1895	113	1936	105	1977	109
1814	--	1855	125	1896	116	1937	117	1978	118
1815	--	1856	116	1897	116	1938	109	1979	113
1816	--	1857	111	1898	108	1939	126	1980	104
1817	--	1858	--	1899	120	1940	127	1981	89
1818	--	1859	120	1900	116	1941	104	1982	118
1819	--	1860	115	1901	105	1942	108	1983	97
1820	--	1861	115	1902	94	1943	117	1984	111
1821	--	1862	126	1903	94	1944	120	1985	94
1822	--	1863	123	1904	122	1945	93	1986	104
1823	--	1864	--	1905	113	1946	101	1987	102
1824	--	1865	--	1906	114	1947	108	1988	103
1825	--	1866	--	1907	120	1948	102	1989	112
1826	--	1867	--	1908	115	1949	100	1990	104
1827	--	1868	--	1909	110	1950	114	1991	98
1828	--	1869	--	1910	95	1951	99	1992	101
1829	--	1870	114	1911	119	1952	111	1993	111
1830	--	1871	106	1912	114	1953	91	1994	113
1831	--	1872	122	1913	108	1954	109	1995	104
1832	--	1873	121	1914	114	1955	107	1996	100
1833	--	1874	134	1915	103	1956	120	1997	114
1834	--	1875	126	1916	113	1957	108	1998	98
1835	--	1876	126	1917	117	1958	107	1999	97
1836	129	1877	110	1918	114	1959	114	2000	97
1837	120	1878	105	1919	101	1960	122	2001	118
1838	117	1879	128	1920	118	1961	121	2002	94
1839	108	1880	112	1921	93	1962	113	2003	116
1840	119	1881	113	1922	107	1963	110	2004	105
1841	120	1882	122	1923	118	1964	117	2005	110
1842	109	1883	121	1924	112	1965	112	2006	90
1843	126	1884	119	1925	99	1966	110	2007	114
1844	111	1885	118	1926	122	1967	119	2008	114
1845	122	1886	114	1927	106	1968	105		
1846	105	1887	126	1928	111	1969	114		
1847	130	1888	132	1929	113	1970	117		

Table 2. Ice-out dates for Aziscohos Lake, Maine.

[--, no data]

Location of lake—Latitude 45°01'16", longitude 71°00'51"

Period of record—1913 to 2008

Years of record—94

Observers—Union Water Power Company, FPL Energy Maine

Year	Julian day	Year	Julian day	Year	Julian day	Year	Julian day	Year	Julian day
1807	--	1848	--	1889	--	1930	125	1971	134
1808	--	1849	--	1890	--	1931	113	1972	141
1809	--	1850	--	1891	--	1932	129	1973	123
1810	--	1851	--	1892	--	1933	131	1974	135
1811	--	1852	--	1893	--	1934	--	1975	133
1812	--	1853	--	1894	--	1935	--	1976	118
1813	--	1854	--	1895	--	1936	122	1977	126
1814	--	1855	--	1896	--	1937	133	1978	136
1815	--	1856	--	1897	--	1938	120	1979	122
1816	--	1857	--	1898	--	1939	133	1980	125
1817	--	1858	--	1899	--	1940	136	1981	121
1818	--	1859	--	1900	--	1941	118	1982	130
1819	--	1860	--	1901	--	1942	125	1983	126
1820	--	1861	--	1902	--	1943	138	1984	123
1821	--	1862	--	1903	--	1944	132	1985	117
1822	--	1863	--	1904	--	1945	104	1986	116
1823	--	1864	--	1905	--	1946	122	1987	110
1824	--	1865	--	1906	--	1947	137	1988	120
1825	--	1866	--	1907	--	1948	116	1989	128
1826	--	1867	--	1908	--	1949	118	1990	124
1827	--	1868	--	1909	--	1950	128	1991	123
1828	--	1869	--	1910	--	1951	122	1992	135
1829	--	1870	--	1911	--	1952	121	1993	123
1830	--	1871	--	1912	--	1953	114	1994	131
1831	--	1872	--	1913	122	1954	128	1995	122
1832	--	1873	--	1914	128	1955	122	1996	131
1833	--	1874	--	1915	116	1956	134	1997	133
1834	--	1875	--	1916	129	1957	121	1998	113
1835	--	1876	--	1917	134	1958	127	1999	122
1836	--	1877	--	1918	119	1959	126	2000	122
1837	--	1878	--	1919	125	1960	123	2001	126
1838	--	1879	--	1920	131	1961	136	2002	117
1839	--	1880	--	1921	106	1962	129	2003	123
1840	--	1881	--	1922	123	1963	127	2004	122
1841	--	1882	--	1923	126	1964	128	2005	127
1842	--	1883	--	1924	130	1965	126	2006	117
1843	--	1884	--	1925	118	1966	137	2007	125
1844	--	1885	--	1926	136	1967	127	2008	124
1845	--	1886	--	1927	112	1968	114		
1846	--	1887	--	1928	135	1969	131		
1847	--	1888	--	1929	131	1970	136		

Table 3. Ice-out dates for China Lake, Maine.
[--, no data]
Location of lake—Latitude 44°26'02", longitude 69°32'44"
Period of record—1874 to 2008
Years of record—82
Observers—The Town Line, Bill Foster, Captain James Allen, Theresa Plaisted

Year	Julian day	Year	Julian day	Year	Julian day	Year	Julian day	Year	Julian day
1807	--	1848	--	1889	--	1930	--	1971	120
1808	--	1849	--	1890	--	1931	--	1972	122
1809	--	1850	--	1891	--	1932	118	1973	98
1810	--	1851	--	1892	--	1933	110	1974	92
1811	--	1852	--	1893	--	1934	119	1975	113
1812	--	1853	--	1894	--	1935	115	1976	102
1813	--	1854	--	1895	--	1936	95	1977	108
1814	--	1855	--	1896	--	1937	110	1978	111
1815	--	1856	--	1897	--	1938	110	1979	102
1816	--	1857	--	1898	--	1939	124	1980	101
1817	--	1858	--	1899	--	1940	--	1981	77
1818	--	1859	--	1900	--	1941	106	1982	112
1819	--	1860	--	1901	--	1942	--	1983	91
1820	--	1861	--	1902	--	1943	--	1984	108
1821	--	1862	--	1903	--	1944	--	1985	96
1822	--	1863	--	1904	--	1945	92	1986	98
1823	--	1864	--	1905	--	1946	--	1987	96
1824	--	1865	--	1906	--	1947	102	1988	97
1825	--	1866	--	1907	--	1948	99	1989	112
1826	--	1867	--	1908	--	1949	96	1990	101
1827	--	1868	--	1909	--	1950	104	1991	98
1828	--	1869	--	1910	--	1951	99	1992	106
1829	--	1870	--	1911	--	1952	110	1993	111
1830	--	1871	--	1912	--	1953	78	1994	110
1831	--	1872	--	1913	--	1954	109	1995	99
1832	--	1873	--	1914	--	1955	103	1996	96
1833	--	1874	112	1915	--	1956	118	1997	113
1834	--	1875	126	1916	--	1957	100	1998	99
1835	--	1876	121	1917	--	1958	106	1999	92
1836	--	1877	106	1918	--	1959	112	2000	95
1837	--	1878	102	1919	--	1960	112	2001	117
1838	--	1879	123	1920	--	1961	120	2002	96
1839	--	1880	112	1921	87	1962	110	2003	111
1840	--	1881	109	1922	--	1963	112	2004	105
1841	--	1882	--	1923	--	1964	112	2005	106
1842	--	1883	119	1924	--	1965	108	2006	88
1843	--	1884	--	1925	--	1966	108	2007	115
1844	--	1885	--	1926	--	1967	119	2008	108
1845	--	1886	--	1927	--	1968	104		
1846	--	1887	--	1928	--	1969	113		
1847	--	1888	--	1929	--	1970	113		

Table 4. Ice-out dates for Cobbosseecontee Lake, Maine.

[--, no data]

Location of lake—Latitude 44°16'18", longitude 69°55'46"

Period of record—1840 to 2008

Years of record—167

Observers—Sara Farr, Mary Oatway, Bill Schenck, Nancy Schenck

Comments—1974 and 1994 were filled in from a secondary observer and adjusted by the average difference in the ice-out dates between the primary and secondary observers.

Year	Julian day	Year	Julian day	Year	Julian day	Year	Julian day	Year	Julian day
1807	--	1848	--	1889	105	1930	103	1971	120
1808	--	1849	--	1890	116	1931	102	1972	120
1809	--	1850	121	1891	118	1932	111	1973	107
1810	--	1851	111	1892	109	1933	109	1974	96
1811	--	1852	124	1893	124	1934	112	1975	115
1812	--	1853	110	1894	114	1935	115	1976	107
1813	--	1854	128	1895	111	1936	103	1977	111
1814	--	1855	115	1896	113	1937	113	1978	117
1815	--	1856	117	1897	114	1938	108	1979	107
1816	--	1857	107	1898	106	1939	124	1980	100
1817	--	1858	108	1899	119	1940	123	1981	75
1818	--	1859	120	1900	114	1941	102	1982	112
1819	--	1860	114	1901	110	1942	103	1983	100
1820	--	1861	115	1902	92	1943	116	1984	107
1821	--	1862	126	1903	95	1944	119	1985	95
1822	--	1863	122	1904	119	1945	93	1986	101
1823	--	1864	114	1905	111	1946	97	1987	101
1824	--	1865	103	1906	114	1947	104	1988	102
1825	--	1866	108	1907	121	1948	100	1989	113
1826	--	1867	117	1908	112	1949	101	1990	104
1827	--	1868	122	1909	109	1950	111	1991	97
1828	--	1869	119	1910	94	1951	96	1992	100
1829	--	1870	114	1911	118	1952	111	1993	111
1830	--	1871	99	1912	115	1953	87	1994	114
1831	--	1872	124	1913	107	1954	109	1995	99
1832	--	1873	122	1914	116	1955	106	1996	98
1833	--	1874	124	1915	104	1956	119	1997	113
1834	--	1875	122	1916	113	1957	103	1998	95
1835	--	1876	122	1917	116	1958	106	1999	94
1836	--	1877	108	1918	118	1959	112	2000	94
1837	--	1878	104	1919	100	1960	115	2001	118
1838	--	1879	125	1920	119	1961	120	2002	94
1839	--	1880	113	1921	91	1962	112	2003	113
1840	106	1881	111	1922	105	1963	111	2004	104
1841	118	1882	118	1923	116	1964	112	2005	107
1842	106	1883	121	1924	110	1965	109	2006	88
1843	125	1884	117	1925	96	1966	109	2007	113
1844	113	1885	119	1926	123	1967	119	2008	114
1845	122	1886	110	1927	106	1968	104		
1846	107	1887	127	1928	111	1969	114		
1847	128	1888	130	1929	111	1970	120		

Table 5. Ice-out dates for Damariscotta Lake, Maine.

[--, no data]

Location of lake—Latitude 44°10'57", longitude 69°28'45"

Period of record—1837 to 2008

Years of record—171

Observers—Fred Jackson and family (three generations), James Birkett, *www.mainelakecharts.com*

Comments— Ice-out for most years is thought to have been observed from the northern end of the lake. Dates for 1959, 1962–68, 1970–78, and 1997–98 were filled in from a secondary observer and adjusted by the average difference in the dates between the primary and secondary observers.

Year	Julian day	Year	Julian day	Year	Julian day	Year	Julian day	Year	Julian day
1807	--	1848	102	1889	102	1930	100	1971	118
1808	--	1849	98	1890	112	1931	101	1972	115
1809	--	1850	118	1891	108	1932	103	1973	96
1810	--	1851	106	1892	102	1933	97	1974	77
1811	--	1852	118	1893	119	1934	107	1975	111
1812	--	1853	103	1894	110	1935	112	1976	99
1813	--	1854	124	1895	111	1936	92	1977	108
1814	--	1855	105	1896	110	1937	108	1978	116
1815	--	1856	117	1897	109	1938	100	1979	97
1816	--	1857	104	1898	102	1939	121	1980	97
1817	--	1858	119	1899	115	1940	118	1981	72
1818	--	1859	100	1900	102	1941	103	1982	112
1819	--	1860	116	1901	108	1942	100	1983	85
1820	--	1861	108	1902	86	1943	112	1984	103
1821	--	1862	122	1903	85	1944	114	1985	93
1822	--	1863	114	1904	117	1945	91	1986	96
1823	--	1864	110	1905	111	1946	90	1987	101
1824	--	1865	97	1906	111	1947	101	1988	97
1825	--	1866	106	1907	120	1948	95	1989	106
1826	--	1867	113	1908	107	1949	96	1990	100
1827	--	1868	122	1909	104	1950	108	1991	96
1828	--	1869	115	1910	92	1951	92	1992	100
1829	--	1870	108	1911	118	1952	108	1993	111
1830	--	1871	86	1912	110	1953	84	1994	106
1831	--	1872	124	1913	95	1954	99	1995	95
1832	--	1873	119	1914	111	1955	101	1996	98
1833	--	1874	116	1915	91	1956	117	1997	111
1834	--	1875	122	1916	109	1957	96	1998	73
1835	--	1876	118	1917	114	1958	99	1999	81
1836	--	1877	105	1918	114	1959	109	2000	94
1837	115	1878	97	1919	95	1960	111	2001	113
1838	110	1879	120	1920	114	1961	119	2002	73
1839	105	1880	108	1921	87	1962	104	2003	107
1840	103	1881	106	1922	102	1963	114	2004	101
1841	115	1882	115	1923	115	1964	112	2005	100
1842	107	1883	118	1924	109	1965	103	2006	86
1843	121	1884	115	1925	93	1966	110	2007	112
1844	105	1885	115	1926	122	1967	121	2008	108
1845	115	1886	114	1927	--	1968	104		
1846	100	1887	124	1928	103	1969	110		
1847	123	1888	126	1929	106	1970	112		

Table 6. Ice-out dates for Eagle Lake, Maine.

[--, no data]

Location of lake—Latitude 47°02'54", longitude 68°35'07"

Period of record—1922 to 2008

Years of record—75

Observers—Maine Department of Inland Fisheries and Wildlife, Derwood Humphrey, S.C. Michaud, John M. Caron

Year	Julian day	Year	Julian day	Year	Julian day	Year	Julian day	Year	Julian day
1807	--	1848	--	1889	--	1930	127	1971	138
1808	--	1849	--	1890	--	1931	114	1972	141
1809	--	1850	--	1891	--	1932	127	1973	129
1810	--	1851	--	1892	--	1933	128	1974	143
1811	--	1852	--	1893	--	1934	122	1975	135
1812	--	1853	--	1894	--	1935	126	1976	124
1813	--	1854	--	1895	--	1936	123	1977	131
1814	--	1855	--	1896	--	1937	127	1978	134
1815	--	1856	--	1897	--	1938	119	1979	124
1816	--	1857	--	1898	--	1939	132	1980	128
1817	--	1858	--	1899	--	1940	134	1981	122
1818	--	1859	--	1900	--	1941	128	1982	134
1819	--	1860	--	1901	--	1942	124	1983	125
1820	--	1861	--	1902	--	1943	138	1984	129
1821	--	1862	--	1903	--	1944	133	1985	128
1822	--	1863	--	1904	--	1945	104	1986	120
1823	--	1864	--	1905	--	1946	133	1987	109
1824	--	1865	--	1906	--	1947	140	1988	123
1825	--	1866	--	1907	--	1948	127	1989	125
1826	--	1867	--	1908	--	1949	123	1990	122
1827	--	1868	--	1909	--	1950	128	1991	--
1828	--	1869	--	1910	--	1951	117	1992	134
1829	--	1870	--	1911	--	1952	128	1993	124
1830	--	1871	--	1912	--	1953	126	1994	--
1831	--	1872	--	1913	--	1954	123	1995	125
1832	--	1873	--	1914	--	1955	124	1996	--
1833	--	1874	--	1915	--	1956	133	1997	125
1834	--	1875	--	1916	--	1957	128	1998	121
1835	--	1876	--	1917	--	1958	115	1999	124
1836	--	1877	--	1918	--	1959	128	2000	125
1837	--	1878	--	1919	--	1960	--	2001	127
1838	--	1879	--	1920	--	1961	--	2002	122
1839	--	1880	--	1921	--	1962	--	2003	132
1840	--	1881	--	1922	115	1963	--	2004	123
1841	--	1882	--	1923	128	1964	--	2005	130
1842	--	1883	--	1924	134	1965	--	2006	119
1843	--	1884	--	1925	124	1966	--	2007	130
1844	--	1885	--	1926	138	1967	--	2008	130
1845	--	1886	--	1927	122	1968	--		
1846	--	1887	--	1928	129	1969	134		
1847	--	1888	--	1929	127	1970	130		

Table 7.   Ice-out dates for Embden Pond, Maine.

[--, no data]

Location of lake—Latitude 44°56'20", longitude 69°57'12"

Period of record—1925 to 2005

Years of record—80

Observer—Maine Department of Inland Fisheries and Wildlife

Year	Julian day	Year	Julian day	Year	Julian day	Year	Julian day	Year	Julian day
1807	--	1848	--	1889	--	1930	113	1971	128
1808	--	1849	--	1890	--	1931	100	1972	133
1809	--	1850	--	1891	--	1932	112	1973	115
1810	--	1851	--	1892	--	1933	120	1974	115
1811	--	1852	--	1893	--	1934	114	1975	124
1812	--	1853	--	1894	--	1935	117	1976	114
1813	--	1854	--	1895	--	1936	115	1977	114
1814	--	1855	--	1896	--	1937	122	1978	125
1815	--	1856	--	1897	--	1938	114	1979	110
1816	--	1857	--	1898	--	1939	129	1980	111
1817	--	1858	--	1899	--	1940	129	1981	95
1818	--	1859	--	1900	--	1941	107	1982	122
1819	--	1860	--	1901	--	1942	118	1983	108
1820	--	1861	--	1902	--	1943	128	1984	118
1821	--	1862	--	1903	--	1944	126	1985	111
1822	--	1863	--	1904	--	1945	102	1986	110
1823	--	1864	--	1905	--	1946	107	1987	105
1824	--	1865	--	1906	--	1947	116	1988	112
1825	--	1866	--	1907	--	1948	106	1989	110
1826	--	1867	--	1908	--	1949	106	1990	117
1827	--	1868	--	1909	--	1950	120	1991	115
1828	--	1869	--	1910	--	1951	109	1992	121
1829	--	1870	--	1911	--	1952	118	1993	121
1830	--	1871	--	1912	--	1953	105	1994	124
1831	--	1872	--	1913	--	1954	117	1995	112
1832	--	1873	--	1914	--	1955	111	1996	115
1833	--	1874	--	1915	--	1956	125	1997	118
1834	--	1875	--	1916	--	1957	113	1998	105
1835	--	1876	--	1917	--	1958	113	1999	104
1836	--	1877	--	1918	--	1959	119	2000	107
1837	--	1878	--	1919	--	1960	120	2001	121
1838	--	1879	--	1920	--	1961	126	2002	--
1839	--	1880	--	1921	--	1962	113	2003	117
1840	--	1881	--	1922	--	1963	114	2004	110
1841	--	1882	--	1923	--	1964	120	2005	112
1842	--	1883	--	1924	--	1965	119		
1843	--	1884	--	1925	109	1966	122		
1844	--	1885	--	1926	127	1967	122		
1845	--	1886	--	1927	108	1968	113		
1846	--	1887	--	1928	128	1969	124		
1847	--	1888	--	1929	120	1970	124		

Table 8. Ice-out dates for First Connecticut Lake, New Hampshire.

[--, no data]

Location of lake—Latitude 45°05'18", longitude 71°14'55"

Period of record—1920 to 2008

Years of record—89

Observers—C. J. Carlson, PG&E National Energy Group, Fred T. Scott, Bob Ward

Year	Julian day	Year	Julian day	Year	Julian day	Year	Julian day	Year	Julian day
1807	--	1848	--	1889	--	1930	126	1971	132
1808	--	1849	--	1890	--	1931	105	1972	140
1809	--	1850	--	1891	--	1932	130	1973	120
1810	--	1851	--	1892	--	1933	127	1974	135
1811	--	1852	--	1893	--	1934	118	1975	132
1812	--	1853	--	1894	--	1935	130	1976	115
1813	--	1854	--	1895	--	1936	123	1977	126
1814	--	1855	--	1896	--	1937	128	1978	136
1815	--	1856	--	1897	--	1938	118	1979	119
1816	--	1857	--	1898	--	1939	131	1980	124
1817	--	1858	--	1899	--	1940	134	1981	118
1818	--	1859	--	1900	--	1941	115	1982	133
1819	--	1860	--	1901	--	1942	123	1983	124
1820	--	1861	--	1902	--	1943	138	1984	120
1821	--	1862	--	1903	--	1944	129	1985	129
1822	--	1863	--	1904	--	1945	103	1986	115
1823	--	1864	--	1905	--	1946	126	1987	110
1824	--	1865	--	1906	--	1947	137	1988	124
1825	--	1866	--	1907	--	1948	118	1989	132
1826	--	1867	--	1908	--	1949	113	1990	122
1827	--	1868	--	1909	--	1950	127	1991	121
1828	--	1869	--	1910	--	1951	119	1992	134
1829	--	1870	--	1911	--	1952	121	1993	122
1830	--	1871	--	1912	--	1953	104	1994	129
1831	--	1872	--	1913	--	1954	122	1995	125
1832	--	1873	--	1914	--	1955	118	1996	134
1833	--	1874	--	1915	--	1956	133	1997	132
1834	--	1875	--	1916	--	1957	121	1998	108
1835	--	1876	--	1917	--	1958	116	1999	124
1836	--	1877	--	1918	--	1959	126	2000	124
1837	--	1878	--	1919	--	1960	122	2001	125
1838	--	1879	--	1920	128	1961	135	2002	116
1839	--	1880	--	1921	99	1962	132	2003	122
1840	--	1881	--	1922	123	1963	126	2004	121
1841	--	1882	--	1923	127	1964	127	2005	120
1842	--	1883	--	1924	128	1965	128	2006	116
1843	--	1884	--	1925	113	1966	134	2007	125
1844	--	1885	--	1926	127	1967	128	2008	122
1845	--	1886	--	1927	113	1968	112		
1846	--	1887	--	1928	131	1969	131		
1847	--	1888	--	1929	129	1970	127		

Table 9.   Ice-out dates for Houghtons (Hoosicwhisick) Pond, Massachusetts.

[--, no data]

Location of lake—Latitude 42°12'26", longitude 71°05'47"

Period of record—1886 to 2008

Years of record—123

Observer—Blue Hills Observatory

Year	Julian day	Year	Julian day	Year	Julian day	Year	Julian day	Year	Julian day
1807	--	1848	--	1889	71	1930	68	1971	90
1808	--	1849	--	1890	71	1931	86	1972	89
1809	--	1850	--	1891	81	1932	89	1973	66
1810	--	1851	--	1892	94	1933	86	1974	63
1811	--	1852	--	1893	91	1934	91	1975	75
1812	--	1853	--	1894	71	1935	85	1976	60
1813	--	1854	--	1895	95	1936	81	1977	83
1814	--	1855	--	1896	93	1937	77	1978	92
1815	--	1856	--	1897	83	1938	77	1979	84
1816	--	1857	--	1898	74	1939	91	1980	78
1817	--	1858	--	1899	97	1940	97	1981	53
1818	--	1859	--	1900	80	1941	95	1982	80
1819	--	1860	--	1901	84	1942	68	1983	70
1820	--	1861	--	1902	76	1943	82	1984	56
1821	--	1862	--	1903	71	1944	86	1985	65
1822	--	1863	--	1904	95	1945	79	1986	72
1823	--	1864	--	1905	92	1946	73	1987	90
1824	--	1865	--	1906	94	1947	74	1988	84
1825	--	1866	--	1907	87	1948	85	1989	76
1826	--	1867	--	1908	86	1949	64	1990	54
1827	--	1868	--	1909	76	1950	89	1991	62
1828	--	1869	--	1910	83	1951	60	1992	68
1829	--	1870	--	1911	88	1952	85	1993	98
1830	--	1871	--	1912	90	1953	58	1994	95
1831	--	1872	--	1913	73	1954	57	1995	73
1832	--	1873	--	1914	92	1955	59	1996	84
1833	--	1874	--	1915	74	1956	98	1997	54
1834	--	1875	--	1916	97	1957	71	1998	55
1835	--	1876	--	1917	96	1958	73	1999	63
1836	--	1877	--	1918	92	1959	79	2000	68
1837	--	1878	--	1919	65	1960	55	2001	94
1838	--	1879	--	1920	96	1961	91	2002	53
1839	--	1880	--	1921	72	1962	86	2003	88
1840	--	1881	--	1922	87	1963	87	2004	73
1841	--	1882	--	1923	99	1964	85	2005	92
1842	--	1883	--	1924	97	1965	76	2006	71
1843	--	1884	--	1925	71	1966	83	2007	74
1844	--	1885	--	1926	104	1967	94	2008	69
1845	--	1886	86	1927	78	1968	89		
1846	--	1887	100	1928	87	1969	95		
1847	--	1888	100	1929	80	1970	80		

Table 10. Ice-out dates for Kezar Lake, Maine.

[--, no data]

Location of lake—Latitude 44°11'04", longitude 70°54'12"

Period of record—1901 to 2008

Years of record—108

Observers—Lovell Town Office, Advertiser Democrat, Arthur P. Stone, Fred and Ruth Mitchell

Year	Julian day	Year	Julian day	Year	Julian day	Year	Julian day	Year	Julian day
1807	--	1848	--	1889	--	1930	104	1971	122
1808	--	1849	--	1890	--	1931	103	1972	124
1809	--	1850	--	1891	--	1932	119	1973	109
1810	--	1851	--	1892	--	1933	119	1974	116
1811	--	1852	--	1893	--	1934	114	1975	121
1812	--	1853	--	1894	--	1935	115	1976	110
1813	--	1854	--	1895	--	1936	113	1977	110
1814	--	1855	--	1896	--	1937	122	1978	122
1815	--	1856	--	1897	--	1938	110	1979	116
1816	--	1857	--	1898	--	1939	126	1980	111
1817	--	1858	--	1899	--	1940	126	1981	97
1818	--	1859	--	1900	--	1941	104	1982	120
1819	--	1860	--	1901	110	1942	114	1983	104
1820	--	1861	--	1902	103	1943	122	1984	112
1821	--	1862	--	1903	109	1944	123	1985	107
1822	--	1863	--	1904	123	1945	99	1986	107
1823	--	1864	--	1905	112	1946	100	1987	103
1824	--	1865	--	1906	98	1947	114	1988	108
1825	--	1866	--	1907	120	1948	105	1989	118
1826	--	1867	--	1908	120	1949	102	1990	113
1827	--	1868	--	1909	117	1950	117	1991	101
1828	--	1869	--	1910	97	1951	110	1992	116
1829	--	1870	--	1911	121	1952	114	1993	118
1830	--	1871	--	1912	116	1953	104	1994	118
1831	--	1872	--	1913	109	1954	112	1995	114
1832	--	1873	--	1914	116	1955	112	1996	111
1833	--	1874	--	1915	107	1956	122	1997	107
1834	--	1875	--	1916	113	1957	107	1998	114
1835	--	1876	--	1917	118	1958	110	1999	100
1836	--	1877	--	1918	113	1959	113	2000	104
1837	--	1878	--	1919	100	1960	115	2001	117
1838	--	1879	--	1920	120	1961	121	2002	100
1839	--	1880	--	1921	93	1962	114	2003	116
1840	--	1881	--	1922	107	1963	113	2004	110
1841	--	1882	--	1923	115	1964	119	2005	108
1842	--	1883	--	1924	113	1965	118	2006	93
1843	--	1884	--	1925	105	1966	113	2007	114
1844	--	1885	--	1926	123	1967	118	2008	115
1845	--	1886	--	1927	106	1968	107		
1846	--	1887	--	1928	126	1969	119		
1847	--	1888	--	1929	115	1970	123		

Table 11. Ice-out dates for Maranacook Lake, Maine.

[--, no data]

Location of lake—Latitude 44°20'03", longitude 69°57'21"

Period of record—1925 to 2008

Years of record—84

Observers—Community Advertiser, John Neff, Roscoe Sprague, Roger Audette, *www.mainelakecharts.com*

Comments—Ice-out for most years is thought to have been observed from the southern end of the lake.

Year	Julian day	Year	Julian day	Year	Julian day	Year	Julian day	Year	Julian day
1807	--	1848	--	1889	--	1930	101	1971	123
1808	--	1849	--	1890	--	1931	101	1972	123
1809	--	1850	--	1891	--	1932	110	1973	107
1810	--	1851	--	1892	--	1933	109	1974	100
1811	--	1852	--	1893	--	1934	110	1975	118
1812	--	1853	--	1894	--	1935	107	1976	106
1813	--	1854	--	1895	--	1936	105	1977	108
1814	--	1855	--	1896	--	1937	116	1978	118
1815	--	1856	--	1897	--	1938	109	1979	107
1816	--	1857	--	1898	--	1939	124	1980	100
1817	--	1858	--	1899	--	1940	123	1981	84
1818	--	1859	--	1900	--	1941	102	1982	115
1819	--	1860	--	1901	--	1942	110	1983	92
1820	--	1861	--	1902	--	1943	116	1984	109
1821	--	1862	--	1903	--	1944	119	1985	97
1822	--	1863	--	1904	--	1945	104	1986	102
1823	--	1864	--	1905	--	1946	101	1987	102
1824	--	1865	--	1906	--	1947	109	1988	101
1825	--	1866	--	1907	--	1948	100	1989	114
1826	--	1867	--	1908	--	1949	100	1990	103
1827	--	1868	--	1909	--	1950	111	1991	97
1828	--	1869	--	1910	--	1951	97	1992	100
1829	--	1870	--	1911	--	1952	111	1993	110
1830	--	1871	--	1912	--	1953	89	1994	113
1831	--	1872	--	1913	--	1954	110	1995	100
1832	--	1873	--	1914	--	1955	105	1996	96
1833	--	1874	--	1915	--	1956	119	1997	115
1834	--	1875	--	1916	--	1957	105	1998	100
1835	--	1876	--	1917	--	1958	106	1999	99
1836	--	1877	--	1918	--	1959	111	2000	100
1837	--	1878	--	1919	--	1960	113	2001	118
1838	--	1879	--	1920	--	1961	121	2002	100
1839	--	1880	--	1921	--	1962	111	2003	114
1840	--	1881	--	1922	--	1963	111	2004	110
1841	--	1882	--	1923	--	1964	112	2005	108
1842	--	1883	--	1924	--	1965	114	2006	89
1843	--	1884	--	1925	105	1966	108	2007	113
1844	--	1885	--	1926	123	1967	118	2008	117
1845	--	1886	--	1927	120	1968	104		
1846	--	1887	--	1928	111	1969	115		
1847	--	1888	--	1929	110	1970	119		

14

Table 12. Ice-out dates for Messalonskee Lake, Maine.

[--, no data]

Location of lake—Latitude 44°28'41", longitude 69°47'34"

Period of record—1909 to 2008

Years of record—75

Observers—Central Maine Morning Sentinel, Joyce Rushton, Sue Alto, *www.mainelakecharts.com*

Year	Julian day	Year	Julian day	Year	Julian day	Year	Julian day	Year	Julian day
1807	--	1848	--	1889	--	1930	113	1971	--
1808	--	1849	--	1890	--	1931	105	1972	--
1809	--	1850	--	1891	--	1932	113	1973	--
1810	--	1851	--	1892	--	1933	115	1974	--
1811	--	1852	--	1893	--	1934	114	1975	--
1812	--	1853	--	1894	--	1935	116	1976	--
1813	--	1854	--	1895	--	1936	107	1977	--
1814	--	1855	--	1896	--	1937	117	1978	--
1815	--	1856	--	1897	--	1938	110	1979	--
1816	--	1857	--	1898	--	1939	127	1980	--
1817	--	1858	--	1899	--	1940	128	1981	--
1818	--	1859	--	1900	--	1941	106	1982	--
1819	--	1860	--	1901	--	1942	112	1983	--
1820	--	1861	--	1902	--	1943	119	1984	--
1821	--	1862	--	1903	--	1944	119	1985	90
1822	--	1863	--	1904	--	1945	--	1986	--
1823	--	1864	--	1905	--	1946	105	1987	102
1824	--	1865	--	1906	--	1947	110	1988	101
1825	--	1866	--	1907	--	1948	107	1989	116
1826	--	1867	--	1908	--	1949	102	1990	109
1827	--	1868	--	1909	114	1950	113	1991	105
1828	--	1869	--	1910	95	1951	110	1992	113
1829	--	1870	--	1911	120	1952	114	1993	113
1830	--	1871	--	1912	115	1953	100	1994	116
1831	--	1872	--	1913	110	1954	113	1995	106
1832	--	1873	--	1914	120	1955	108	1996	108
1833	--	1874	--	1915	105	1956	122	1997	116
1834	--	1875	--	1916	--	1957	108	1998	100
1835	--	1876	--	1917	118	1958	108	1999	99
1836	--	1877	--	1918	114	1959	114	2000	100
1837	--	1878	--	1919	103	1960	119	2001	120
1838	--	1879	--	1920	121	1961	123	2002	100
1839	--	1880	--	1921	97	1962	113	2003	117
1840	--	1881	--	1922	105	1963	--	2004	110
1841	--	1882	--	1923	115	1964	--	2005	109
1842	--	1883	--	1924	111	1965	--	2006	93
1843	--	1884	--	1925	100	1966	--	2007	117
1844	--	1885	--	1926	123	1967	--	2008	114
1845	--	1886	--	1927	106	1968	--		
1846	--	1887	--	1928	120	1969	--		
1847	--	1888	--	1929	115	1970	--		

Table 13. Ice-out dates for Moosehead Lake, Maine.

[--, no data]

Location of lake—Latitude 45°38'27", longitude 69°39'57"

Period of record—1848 to 2008

Years of record—161

Observers—Kennebec Water Power Company, Maine Department of Inland Fisheries and Wildlife, Roger Currier

Comments—Ice-out definition for most years is thought to have been the earliest date of open navigation from Greenville to Northeast Carry.

Year	Julian day	Year	Julian day	Year	Julian day	Year	Julian day	Year	Julian day
1807	--	1848	121	1889	120	1930	125	1971	134
1808	--	1849	132	1890	129	1931	114	1972	143
1809	--	1850	129	1891	134	1932	126	1973	125
1810	--	1851	134	1892	125	1933	124	1974	136
1811	--	1852	138	1893	138	1934	124	1975	132
1812	--	1853	131	1894	121	1935	130	1976	122
1813	--	1854	140	1895	126	1936	123	1977	126
1814	--	1855	137	1896	129	1937	130	1978	135
1815	--	1856	130	1897	128	1938	119	1979	121
1816	--	1857	132	1898	124	1939	137	1980	123
1817	--	1858	133	1899	127	1940	138	1981	117
1818	--	1859	134	1900	131	1941	119	1982	133
1819	--	1860	132	1901	119	1942	125	1983	122
1820	--	1861	132	1902	118	1943	138	1984	127
1821	--	1862	138	1903	118	1944	135	1985	123
1822	--	1863	138	1904	131	1945	104	1986	118
1823	--	1864	127	1905	122	1946	126	1987	111
1824	--	1865	124	1906	133	1947	133	1988	124
1825	--	1866	131	1907	134	1948	125	1989	132
1826	--	1867	139	1908	132	1949	113	1990	127
1827	--	1868	139	1909	135	1950	127	1991	122
1828	--	1869	130	1910	110	1951	119	1992	134
1829	--	1870	124	1911	133	1952	121	1993	128
1830	--	1871	133	1912	129	1953	114	1994	131
1831	--	1872	132	1913	122	1954	122	1995	122
1832	--	1873	136	1914	135	1955	124	1996	126
1833	--	1874	146	1915	121	1956	136	1997	131
1834	--	1875	144	1916	125	1957	122	1998	117
1835	--	1876	144	1917	134	1958	122	1999	120
1836	--	1877	126	1918	121	1959	129	2000	121
1837	--	1878	149	1919	123	1960	127	2001	124
1838	--	1879	134	1920	135	1961	137	2002	110
1839	--	1880	127	1921	112	1962	138	2003	127
1840	--	1881	129	1922	121	1963	127	2004	122
1841	--	1882	138	1923	130	1964	128	2005	130
1842	--	1883	133	1924	130	1965	127	2006	109
1843	--	1884	129	1925	118	1966	126	2007	132
1844	--	1885	136	1926	138	1967	128	2008	128
1845	--	1886	122	1927	115	1968	116		
1846	--	1887	133	1928	133	1969	133		
1847	--	1888	143	1929	128	1970	136		

Table 14. Ice-out dates for Mooselookmeguntic Lake, Maine.

[--, no data]

Location of lake—Latitude 44°54'25", longitude 70°48'40"

Period of record—1884 to 2008

Years of record—107

Observers—Union Water Power Company, FPL Energy Maine

Year	Julian day	Year	Julian day	Year	Julian day	Year	Julian day	Year	Julian day
1807	--	1848	--	1889	--	1930	126	1971	133
1808	--	1849	--	1890	131	1931	116	1972	143
1809	--	1850	--	1891	130	1932	127	1973	124
1810	--	1851	--	1892	127	1933	127	1974	135
1811	--	1852	--	1893	141	1934	--	1975	133
1812	--	1853	--	1894	--	1935	--	1976	120
1813	--	1854	--	1895	--	1936	125	1977	125
1814	--	1855	--	1896	--	1937	133	1978	136
1815	--	1856	--	1897	133	1938	118	1979	122
1816	--	1857	--	1898	124	1939	135	1980	124
1817	--	1858	--	1899	128	1940	138	1981	119
1818	--	1859	--	1900	--	1941	117	1982	134
1819	--	1860	--	1901	--	1942	125	1983	127
1820	--	1861	--	1902	--	1943	140	1984	123
1821	--	1862	--	1903	--	1944	131	1985	128
1822	--	1863	--	1904	--	1945	104	1986	116
1823	--	1864	--	1905	--	1946	121	1987	111
1824	--	1865	--	1906	133	1947	134	1988	124
1825	--	1866	--	1907	--	1948	122	1989	130
1826	--	1867	--	1908	--	1949	118	1990	125
1827	--	1868	--	1909	--	1950	128	1991	121
1828	--	1869	--	1910	108	1951	122	1992	134
1829	--	1870	--	1911	130	1952	123	1993	123
1830	--	1871	--	1912	127	1953	113	1994	130
1831	--	1872	--	1913	124	1954	127	1995	125
1832	--	1873	--	1914	135	1955	120	1996	131
1833	--	1874	--	1915	119	1956	135	1997	131
1834	--	1875	--	1916	129	1957	120	1998	112
1835	--	1876	--	1917	137	1958	122	1999	123
1836	--	1877	--	1918	124	1959	127	2000	121
1837	--	1878	--	1919	123	1960	126	2001	125
1838	--	1879	--	1920	139	1961	135	2002	112
1839	--	1880	--	1921	105	1962	131	2003	124
1840	--	1881	--	1922	125	1963	125	2004	124
1841	--	1882	--	1923	129	1964	127	2005	125
1842	--	1883	--	1924	132	1965	127	2006	112
1843	--	1884	132	1925	118	1966	136	2007	127
1844	--	1885	130	1926	136	1967	129	2008	122
1845	--	1886	--	1927	117	1968	114		
1846	--	1887	--	1928	134	1969	132		
1847	--	1888	--	1929	128	1970	136		

Table 15. Ice-out dates for Pennesseewassee (Norway) Lake, Maine.

[--, no data]

Location of lake—Latitude 44°13'34", longitude 70°34'43"

Period of record—1874 to 2008

Years of record—133

Observer—Woodman's Sporting Goods, Advertiser Democrat

Year	Julian day	Year	Julian day	Year	Julian day	Year	Julian day	Year	Julian day
1807	--	1848	--	1889	106	1930	104	1971	123
1808	--	1849	--	1890	116	1931	102	1972	126
1809	--	1850	--	1891	118	1932	112	1973	112
1810	--	1851	--	1892	109	1933	118	1974	111
1811	--	1852	--	1893	128	1934	113	1975	121
1812	--	1853	--	1894	114	1935	115	1976	109
1813	--	1854	--	1895	111	1936	112	1977	109
1814	--	1855	--	1896	118	1937	121	1978	123
1815	--	1856	--	1897	117	1938	110	1979	116
1816	--	1857	--	1898	108	1939	127	1980	104
1817	--	1858	--	1899	119	1940	128	1981	91
1818	--	1859	--	1900	119	1941	125	1982	120
1819	--	1860	--	1901	111	1942	111	1983	99
1820	--	1861	--	1902	106	1943	118	1984	112
1821	--	1862	--	1903	101	1944	123	1985	102
1822	--	1863	--	1904	124	1945	99	1986	107
1823	--	1864	--	1905	112	1946	100	1987	107
1824	--	1865	--	1906	116	1947	113	1988	101
1825	--	1866	--	1907	120	1948	101	1989	116
1826	--	1867	--	1908	117	1949	101	1990	101
1827	--	1868	--	1909	117	1950	117	1991	101
1828	--	1869	--	1910	96	1951	105	1992	113
1829	--	1870	--	1911	119	1952	111	1993	112
1830	--	1871	--	1912	116	1953	100	1994	116
1831	--	1872	--	1913	113	1954	113	1995	102
1832	--	1873	--	1914	116	1955	110	1996	--
1833	--	1874	133	1915	105	1956	123	1997	117
1834	--	1875	126	1916	112	1957	107	1998	110
1835	--	1876	132	1917	118	1958	109	1999	113
1836	--	1877	112	1918	114	1959	114	2000	--
1837	--	1878	102	1919	104	1960	116	2001	121
1838	--	1879	127	1920	124	1961	120	2002	100
1839	--	1880	113	1921	98	1962	113	2003	113
1840	--	1881	119	1922	109	1963	111	2004	110
1841	--	1882	121	1923	119	1964	118	2005	109
1842	--	1883	122	1924	112	1965	114	2006	90
1843	--	1884	117	1925	104	1966	113	2007	114
1844	--	1885	122	1926	123	1967	118	2008	115
1845	--	1886	114	1927	106	1968	105		
1846	--	1887	126	1928	118	1969	117		
1847	--	1888	131	1929	116	1970	121		

Table 16. Ice-out dates for Ponkapoag Pond, Massachusetts.

[--, no data]

Location of lake—Latitude 42°11'31", longitude 71°05'40"

Period of record—1886 to 2008

Years of record—123

Observer—Blue Hills Observatory

Year	Julian day	Year	Julian day	Year	Julian day	Year	Julian day	Year	Julian day
1807	--	1848	--	1889	71	1930	67	1971	87
1808	--	1849	--	1890	71	1931	84	1972	83
1809	--	1850	--	1891	72	1932	89	1973	66
1810	--	1851	--	1892	93	1933	82	1974	63
1811	--	1852	--	1893	91	1934	88	1975	75
1812	--	1853	--	1894	71	1935	83	1976	60
1813	--	1854	--	1895	86	1936	80	1977	75
1814	--	1855	--	1896	93	1937	77	1978	92
1815	--	1856	--	1897	82	1938	77	1979	82
1816	--	1857	--	1898	73	1939	88	1980	71
1817	--	1858	--	1899	90	1940	97	1981	52
1818	--	1859	--	1900	79	1941	92	1982	74
1819	--	1860	--	1901	82	1942	68	1983	67
1820	--	1861	--	1902	73	1943	80	1984	52
1821	--	1862	--	1903	70	1944	86	1985	59
1822	--	1863	--	1904	94	1945	79	1986	66
1823	--	1864	--	1905	90	1946	68	1987	89
1824	--	1865	--	1906	90	1947	73	1988	70
1825	--	1866	--	1907	86	1948	84	1989	54
1826	--	1867	--	1908	77	1949	59	1990	41
1827	--	1868	--	1909	76	1950	83	1991	52
1828	--	1869	--	1910	81	1951	54	1992	58
1829	--	1870	--	1911	87	1952	85	1993	94
1830	--	1871	--	1912	82	1953	32	1994	93
1831	--	1872	--	1913	73	1954	53	1995	68
1832	--	1873	--	1914	90	1955	57	1996	57
1833	--	1874	--	1915	71	1956	72	1997	51
1834	--	1875	--	1916	96	1957	58	1998	43
1835	--	1876	--	1917	92	1958	69	1999	36
1836	--	1877	--	1918	91	1959	50	2000	63
1837	--	1878	--	1919	65	1960	54	2001	84
1838	--	1879	--	1920	94	1961	88	2002	50
1839	--	1880	--	1921	69	1962	84	2003	85
1840	--	1881	--	1922	85	1963	86	2004	66
1841	--	1882	--	1923	99	1964	77	2005	92
1842	--	1883	--	1924	96	1965	72	2006	69
1843	--	1884	--	1925	69	1966	80	2007	73
1844	--	1885	--	1926	100	1967	94	2008	69
1845	--	1886	86	1927	76	1968	86		
1846	--	1887	83	1928	85	1969	93		
1847	--	1888	89	1929	79	1970	76		

Table 17. Ice-out dates for Pontoosuc Lake, Massachusetts.

[--, no data]

Location of lake—Latitude 42°29'44", longitude 73°14'59"

Period of record—1925 to 1998

Years of record—74

Observer—Berkshire Eagle

Year	Julian day	Year	Julian day	Year	Julian day	Year	Julian day	Year	Julian day
1807	--	1848	--	1889	--	1930	93	1971	115
1808	--	1849	--	1890	--	1931	100	1972	118
1809	--	1850	--	1891	--	1932	112	1973	90
1810	--	1851	--	1892	--	1933	107	1974	95
1811	--	1852	--	1893	--	1934	108	1975	112
1812	--	1853	--	1894	--	1935	100	1976	94
1813	--	1854	--	1895	--	1936	92	1977	104
1814	--	1855	--	1896	--	1937	105	1978	109
1815	--	1856	--	1897	--	1938	87	1979	111
1816	--	1857	--	1898	--	1939	113	1980	98
1817	--	1858	--	1899	--	1940	121	1981	92
1818	--	1859	--	1900	--	1941	105	1982	112
1819	--	1860	--	1901	--	1942	98	1983	92
1820	--	1861	--	1902	--	1943	116	1984	105
1821	--	1862	--	1903	--	1944	110	1985	92
1822	--	1863	--	1904	--	1945	89	1986	94
1823	--	1864	--	1905	--	1946	86	1987	95
1824	--	1865	--	1906	--	1947	104	1988	100
1825	--	1866	--	1907	--	1948	92	1989	88
1826	--	1867	--	1908	--	1949	87	1990	93
1827	--	1868	--	1909	--	1950	99	1991	86
1828	--	1869	--	1910	--	1951	100	1992	102
1829	--	1870	--	1911	--	1952	102	1993	107
1830	--	1871	--	1912	--	1953	86	1994	108
1831	--	1872	--	1913	--	1954	87	1995	85
1832	--	1873	--	1914	--	1955	105	1996	102
1833	--	1874	--	1915	--	1956	120	1997	99
1834	--	1875	--	1916	--	1957	90	1998	90
1835	--	1876	--	1917	--	1958	105	1999	--
1836	--	1877	--	1918	--	1959	108	2000	--
1837	--	1878	--	1919	--	1960	107	2001	--
1838	--	1879	--	1920	--	1961	111	2002	--
1839	--	1880	--	1921	--	1962	102	2003	--
1840	--	1881	--	1922	--	1963	106	2004	--
1841	--	1882	--	1923	--	1964	108	2005	--
1842	--	1883	--	1924	--	1965	108	2006	--
1843	--	1884	--	1925	92	1966	109	2007	--
1844	--	1885	--	1926	114	1967	110	2008	--
1845	--	1886	--	1927	98	1968	97		
1846	--	1887	--	1928	98	1969	106		
1847	--	1888	--	1929	97	1970	114		

Table 18. Ice-out dates for Portage Lake, Maine.

[--, no data]

Location of lake—Latitude 46°46'17", longitude 68°30'04"

Period of record—1925 to 2008

Years of record—83

Observer—Portage Lake Town Office

Year	Julian day	Year	Julian day	Year	Julian day	Year	Julian day	Year	Julian day
1807	--	1848	--	1889	--	1930	127	1971	133
1808	--	1849	--	1890	--	1931	121	1972	140
1809	--	1850	--	1891	--	1932	129	1973	127
1810	--	1851	--	1892	--	1933	127	1974	141
1811	--	1852	--	1893	--	1934	120	1975	135
1812	--	1853	--	1894	--	1935	132	1976	123
1813	--	1854	--	1895	--	1936	124	1977	132
1814	--	1855	--	1896	--	1937	133	1978	132
1815	--	1856	--	1897	--	1938	118	1979	123
1816	--	1857	--	1898	--	1939	133	1980	125
1817	--	1858	--	1899	--	1940	132	1981	121
1818	--	1859	--	1900	--	1941	122	1982	129
1819	--	1860	--	1901	--	1942	124	1983	121
1820	--	1861	--	1902	--	1943	139	1984	129
1821	--	1862	--	1903	--	1944	129	1985	126
1822	--	1863	--	1904	--	1945	104	1986	118
1823	--	1864	--	1905	--	1946	131	1987	110
1824	--	1865	--	1906	--	1947	138	1988	119
1825	--	1866	--	1907	--	1948	126	1989	125
1826	--	1867	--	1908	--	1949	124	1990	120
1827	--	1868	--	1909	--	1950	127	1991	125
1828	--	1869	--	1910	--	1951	119	1992	132
1829	--	1870	--	1911	--	1952	129	1993	123
1830	--	1871	--	1912	--	1953	125	1994	132
1831	--	1872	--	1913	--	1954	122	1995	124
1832	--	1873	--	1914	--	1955	123	1996	124
1833	--	1874	--	1915	--	1956	133	1997	126
1834	--	1875	--	1916	--	1957	122	1998	120
1835	--	1876	--	1917	--	1958	--	1999	123
1836	--	1877	--	1918	--	1959	129	2000	121
1837	--	1878	--	1919	--	1960	127	2001	125
1838	--	1879	--	1920	--	1961	135	2002	117
1839	--	1880	--	1921	--	1962	130	2003	127
1840	--	1881	--	1922	--	1963	131	2004	118
1841	--	1882	--	1923	--	1964	127	2005	127
1842	--	1883	--	1924	--	1965	124	2006	115
1843	--	1884	--	1925	130	1966	129	2007	130
1844	--	1885	--	1926	146	1967	127	2008	125
1845	--	1886	--	1927	120	1968	123		
1846	--	1887	--	1928	137	1969	131		
1847	--	1888	--	1929	130	1970	133		

Table 19.   Ice-out dates for Rangeley Lake, Maine.

[--, no data]

Location of lake—Latitude 44°56'41", longitude 70°41'54"

Period of record—1880 to 2008

Years of record—129

Observers—Union Water Power Company, FPL Energy Maine

Year	Julian day	Year	Julian day	Year	Julian day	Year	Julian day	Year	Julian day
1807	--	1848	--	1889	120	1930	126	1971	135
1808	--	1849	--	1890	129	1931	116	1972	144
1809	--	1850	--	1891	134	1932	127	1973	124
1810	--	1851	--	1892	130	1933	127	1974	135
1811	--	1852	--	1893	137	1934	125	1975	132
1812	--	1853	--	1894	122	1935	131	1976	119
1813	--	1854	--	1895	127	1936	125	1977	127
1814	--	1855	--	1896	131	1937	131	1978	137
1815	--	1856	--	1897	133	1938	119	1979	121
1816	--	1857	--	1898	125	1939	134	1980	126
1817	--	1858	--	1899	128	1940	140	1981	120
1818	--	1859	--	1900	136	1941	116	1982	133
1819	--	1860	--	1901	124	1942	125	1983	126
1820	--	1861	--	1902	118	1943	140	1984	125
1821	--	1862	--	1903	117	1944	132	1985	130
1822	--	1863	--	1904	135	1945	104	1986	117
1823	--	1864	--	1905	125	1946	122	1987	111
1824	--	1865	--	1906	133	1947	133	1988	126
1825	--	1866	--	1907	139	1948	122	1989	131
1826	--	1867	--	1908	131	1949	114	1990	125
1827	--	1868	--	1909	132	1950	128	1991	121
1828	--	1869	--	1910	109	1951	122	1992	133
1829	--	1870	--	1911	131	1952	123	1993	122
1830	--	1871	--	1912	130	1953	114	1994	128
1831	--	1872	--	1913	124	1954	126	1995	125
1832	--	1873	--	1914	141	1955	120	1996	130
1833	--	1874	--	1915	119	1956	136	1997	133
1834	--	1875	--	1916	129	1957	121	1998	113
1835	--	1876	--	1917	137	1958	127	1999	123
1836	--	1877	--	1918	123	1959	128	2000	121
1837	--	1878	--	1919	123	1960	125	2001	126
1838	--	1879	--	1920	140	1961	135	2002	115
1839	--	1880	134	1921	104	1962	137	2003	126
1840	--	1881	136	1922	124	1963	127	2004	124
1841	--	1882	144	1923	129	1964	127	2005	127
1842	--	1883	136	1924	131	1965	129	2006	113
1843	--	1884	134	1925	119	1966	137	2007	131
1844	--	1885	136	1926	138	1967	130	2008	125
1845	--	1886	124	1927	119	1968	116		
1846	--	1887	137	1928	134	1969	132		
1847	--	1888	142	1929	130	1970	135		

Table 20. Ice-out dates for Richardson Lake, Maine.

[--, no data]

Location of lake—Latitude 44°51'23", longitude 70°51'56"

Period of record—1880 to 2008

Years of record—127

Observers—Union Water Power Company, FPL Energy Maine

Year	Julian day	Year	Julian day	Year	Julian day	Year	Julian day	Year	Julian day
1807	--	1848	--	1889	119	1930	125	1971	132
1808	--	1849	--	1890	131	1931	114	1972	141
1809	--	1850	--	1891	126	1932	125	1973	124
1810	--	1851	--	1892	127	1933	127	1974	133
1811	--	1852	--	1893	141	1934	124	1975	130
1812	--	1853	--	1894	121	1935	131	1976	116
1813	--	1854	--	1895	125	1936	124	1977	125
1814	--	1855	--	1896	130	1937	133	1978	136
1815	--	1856	--	1897	132	1938	--	1979	119
1816	--	1857	--	1898	121	1939	134	1980	124
1817	--	1858	--	1899	128	1940	--	1981	117
1818	--	1859	--	1900	130	1941	116	1982	131
1819	--	1860	--	1901	121	1942	123	1983	126
1820	--	1861	--	1902	113	1943	139	1984	123
1821	--	1862	--	1903	117	1944	130	1985	127
1822	--	1863	--	1904	130	1945	104	1986	115
1823	--	1864	--	1905	123	1946	122	1987	110
1824	--	1865	--	1906	136	1947	133	1988	120
1825	--	1866	--	1907	137	1948	117	1989	131
1826	--	1867	--	1908	128	1949	117	1990	125
1827	--	1868	--	1909	131	1950	127	1991	121
1828	--	1869	--	1910	107	1951	123	1992	134
1829	--	1870	--	1911	130	1952	121	1993	122
1830	--	1871	--	1912	128	1953	112	1994	129
1831	--	1872	--	1913	123	1954	122	1995	126
1832	--	1873	--	1914	136	1955	119	1996	129
1833	--	1874	--	1915	118	1956	135	1997	128
1834	--	1875	--	1916	129	1957	121	1998	109
1835	--	1876	--	1917	137	1958	122	1999	122
1836	--	1877	--	1918	120	1959	125	2000	121
1837	--	1878	--	1919	123	1960	122	2001	125
1838	--	1879	--	1920	138	1961	135	2002	112
1839	--	1880	129	1921	105	1962	129	2003	123
1840	--	1881	135	1922	124	1963	125	2004	123
1841	--	1882	141	1923	127	1964	127	2005	125
1842	--	1883	134	1924	129	1965	127	2006	110
1843	--	1884	133	1925	118	1966	129	2007	128
1844	--	1885	133	1926	135	1967	129	2008	119
1845	--	1886	122	1927	112	1968	114		
1846	--	1887	132	1928	132	1969	130		
1847	--	1888	144	1929	129	1970	134		

Table 21. Ice-out dates for Sebago Lake, Maine.

[--, no data; NCIC, no complete ice cover]

Location of lake—Latitude 43°52'15", longitude 70°34'01"

Period of record—1807 to 2008

Years of record—168

Observers—Maine Sunday Telegram, Carroll Cutting, Portland Press Herald, *www.mainelakecharts.com*

Comments—Ice-out date is thought to have been observed on Big Bay for many years.

Year	Julian day	Year	Julian day	Year	Julian day	Year	Julian day	Year	Julian day
1807	127	1848	--	1889	102	1930	97	1971	122
1808	--	1849	119	1890	114	1931	102	1972	122
1809	--	1850	--	1891	113	1932	73	1973	100
1810	--	1851	110	1892	102	1933	100	1974	101
1811	--	1852	125	1893	124	1934	110	1975	88
1812	122	1853	110	1894	109	1935	107	1976	94
1813	--	1854	--	1895	111	1936	87	1977	94
1814	--	1855	117	1896	112	1937	NCIC	1978	104
1815	--	1856	118	1897	112	1938	92	1979	85
1816	121	1857	104	1898	103	1939	113	1980	102
1817	--	1858	106	1899	117	1940	124	1981	76
1818	--	1859	--	1900	116	1941	102	1982	111
1819	119	1860	--	1901	105	1942	98	1983	76
1820	116	1861	--	1902	89	1943	107	1984	107
1821	119	1862	119	1903	87	1944	115	1985	73
1822	102	1863	118	1904	114	1945	91	1986	90
1823	113	1864	--	1905	115	1946	85	1987	88
1824	108	1865	--	1906	112	1947	NCIC	1988	92
1825	106	1866	108	1907	120	1948	94	1989	100
1826	108	1867	116	1908	116	1949	NCIC	1990	95
1827	--	1868	--	1909	105	1950	107	1991	NCIC
1828	--	1869	--	1910	93	1951	NCIC	1992	87
1829	--	1870	--	1911	119	1952	106	1993	109
1830	--	1871	95	1912	114	1953	NCIC	1994	110
1831	--	1872	125	1913	99	1954	103	1995	77
1832	--	1873	121	1914	110	1955	--	1996	95
1833	--	1874	127	1915	102	1956	97	1997	104
1834	104	1875	126	1916	109	1957	99	1998	NCIC
1835	--	1876	122	1917	114	1958	96	1999	NCIC
1836	--	1877	113	1918	116	1959	96	2000	89
1837	121	1878	102	1919	91	1960	--	2001	114
1838	--	1879	125	1920	114	1961	NCIC	2002	NCIC
1839	--	1880	104	1921	87	1962	100	2003	114
1840	110	1881	114	1922	104	1963	105	2004	100
1841	119	1882	109	1923	112	1964	107	2005	107
1842	110	1883	119	1924	107	1965	104	2006	84
1843	122	1884	117	1925	94	1966	92	2007	113
1844	108	1885	116	1926	120	1967	100	2008	112
1845	114	1886	115	1927	105	1968	99		
1846	104	1887	121	1928	99	1969	111		
1847	--	1888	129	1929	100	1970	113		

Table 22. Ice-out dates for Sebec Lake, Maine.

[--, no data]

Location of lake—Latitude 45°16'58", longitude 69°16'45"

Period of record—1879 to 2008

Years of record—128

Observers—Bill Elliot, Bill Larabee, Ruth Weatherbee

Comments—Ice-out definition for most years is thought to have been the earliest date of open navigation from one end of lake to the other.

Year	Julian day	Year	Julian day	Year	Julian day	Year	Julian day	Year	Julian day
1807	--	1848	--	1889	114	1930	121	1971	127
1808	--	1849	--	1890	--	1931	104	1972	135
1809	--	1850	--	1891	116	1932	118	1973	117
1810	--	1851	--	1892	121	1933	121	1974	121
1811	--	1852	--	1893	132	1934	116	1975	125
1812	--	1853	--	1894	118	1935	118	1976	119
1813	--	1854	--	1895	119	1936	119	1977	118
1814	--	1855	--	1896	125	1937	125	1978	128
1815	--	1856	--	1897	124	1938	117	1979	118
1816	--	1857	--	1898	118	1939	131	1980	115
1817	--	1858	--	1899	124	1940	131	1981	104
1818	--	1859	--	1900	121	1941	112	1982	126
1819	--	1860	--	1901	112	1942	119	1983	110
1820	--	1861	--	1902	91	1943	128	1984	119
1821	--	1862	--	1903	107	1944	126	1985	117
1822	--	1863	--	1904	--	1945	100	1986	114
1823	--	1864	--	1905	119	1946	117	1987	103
1824	--	1865	--	1906	128	1947	126	1988	115
1825	--	1866	--	1907	125	1948	121	1989	123
1826	--	1867	--	1908	126	1949	105	1990	121
1827	--	1868	--	1909	129	1950	122	1991	120
1828	--	1869	--	1910	110	1951	111	1992	128
1829	--	1870	--	1911	126	1952	115	1993	122
1830	--	1871	--	1912	125	1953	107	1994	122
1831	--	1872	--	1913	117	1954	120	1995	114
1832	--	1873	--	1914	129	1955	121	1996	117
1833	--	1874	--	1915	115	1956	127	1997	122
1834	--	1875	--	1916	116	1957	117	1998	108
1835	--	1876	--	1917	127	1958	114	1999	108
1836	--	1877	--	1918	116	1959	118	2000	111
1837	--	1878	--	1919	114	1960	123	2001	122
1838	--	1879	128	1920	129	1961	123	2002	108
1839	--	1880	127	1921	107	1962	124	2003	123
1840	--	1881	118	1922	111	1963	118	2004	112
1841	--	1882	128	1923	126	1964	122	2005	114
1842	--	1883	124	1924	120	1965	121	2006	106
1843	--	1884	119	1925	113	1966	116	2007	122
1844	--	1885	131	1926	130	1967	124	2008	120
1845	--	1886	122	1927	111	1968	119		
1846	--	1887	118	1928	129	1969	125		
1847	--	1888	133	1929	123	1970	127		

Table 23. Ice-out dates for Squa Pan Lake, Maine.

[--, no data]

Location of lake—Latitude 46°33'21", longitude 68°18'24"

Period of record—1930 to 2008

Years of record—70

Observers—Maine Public Service Company, WPS New England Generation, Maine Department of Inland Fisheries and Wildlife

Year	Julian day	Year	Julian day	Year	Julian day	Year	Julian day	Year	Julian day
1807	--	1848	--	1889	--	1930	126	1971	132
1808	--	1849	--	1890	--	1931	112	1972	138
1809	--	1850	--	1891	--	1932	--	1973	124
1810	--	1851	--	1892	--	1933	125	1974	135
1811	--	1852	--	1893	--	1934	118	1975	132
1812	--	1853	--	1894	--	1935	--	1976	120
1813	--	1854	--	1895	--	1936	--	1977	126
1814	--	1855	--	1896	--	1937	123	1978	129
1815	--	1856	--	1897	--	1938	116	1979	119
1816	--	1857	--	1898	--	1939	131	1980	123
1817	--	1858	--	1899	--	1940	128	1981	119
1818	--	1859	--	1900	--	1941	121	1982	128
1819	--	1860	--	1901	--	1942	--	1983	116
1820	--	1861	--	1902	--	1943	136	1984	122
1821	--	1862	--	1903	--	1944	--	1985	119
1822	--	1863	--	1904	--	1945	103	1986	113
1823	--	1864	--	1905	--	1946	126	1987	107
1824	--	1865	--	1906	--	1947	132	1988	117
1825	--	1866	--	1907	--	1948	108	1989	123
1826	--	1867	--	1908	--	1949	114	1990	121
1827	--	1868	--	1909	--	1950	125	1991	123
1828	--	1869	--	1910	--	1951	115	1992	130
1829	--	1870	--	1911	--	1952	122	1993	122
1830	--	1871	--	1912	--	1953	116	1994	127
1831	--	1872	--	1913	--	1954	119	1995	122
1832	--	1873	--	1914	--	1955	120	1996	120
1833	--	1874	--	1915	--	1956	127	1997	125
1834	--	1875	--	1916	--	1957	124	1998	118
1835	--	1876	--	1917	--	1958	119	1999	120
1836	--	1877	--	1918	--	1959	128	2000	--
1837	--	1878	--	1919	--	1960	129	2001	124
1838	--	1879	--	1920	--	1961	136	2002	--
1839	--	1880	--	1921	--	1962	128	2003	126
1840	--	1881	--	1922	--	1963	126	2004	113
1841	--	1882	--	1923	--	1964	123	2005	121
1842	--	1883	--	1924	--	1965	122	2006	109
1843	--	1884	--	1925	--	1966	117	2007	--
1844	--	1885	--	1926	--	1967	--	2008	128
1845	--	1886	--	1927	--	1968	116		
1846	--	1887	--	1928	--	1969	125		
1847	--	1888	--	1929	--	1970	128		

Table 24. Ice-out dates for Sunapee Lake, New Hampshire.

[--, no data]

Location of lake—Latitude 43°23'45", longitude 72°03'11"

Period of record—1869 to 2008

Years of record—140

Observer—Argus Champion, Sunapee Town Office

Year	Julian day	Year	Julian day	Year	Julian day	Year	Julian day	Year	Julian day
1807	--	1848	--	1889	110	1930	107	1971	125
1808	--	1849	--	1890	116	1931	106	1972	127
1809	--	1850	--	1891	114	1932	117	1973	109
1810	--	1851	--	1892	107	1933	120	1974	110
1811	--	1852	--	1893	133	1934	114	1975	125
1812	--	1853	--	1894	109	1935	115	1976	107
1813	--	1854	--	1895	120	1936	105	1977	109
1814	--	1855	--	1896	119	1937	122	1978	121
1815	--	1856	--	1897	119	1938	108	1979	118
1816	--	1857	--	1898	108	1939	127	1980	111
1817	--	1858	--	1899	123	1940	128	1981	99
1818	--	1859	--	1900	120	1941	108	1982	118
1819	--	1860	--	1901	114	1942	109	1983	106
1820	--	1861	--	1902	102	1943	123	1984	112
1821	--	1862	--	1903	95	1944	122	1985	106
1822	--	1863	--	1904	122	1945	91	1986	105
1823	--	1864	--	1905	115	1946	88	1987	103
1824	--	1865	--	1906	119	1947	117	1988	107
1825	--	1866	--	1907	121	1948	99	1989	111
1826	--	1867	--	1908	117	1949	96	1990	106
1827	--	1868	--	1909	112	1950	116	1991	98
1828	--	1869	130	1910	96	1951	110	1992	114
1829	--	1870	130	1911	122	1952	111	1993	112
1830	--	1871	102	1912	117	1953	99	1994	110
1831	--	1872	124	1913	107	1954	106	1995	104
1832	--	1873	126	1914	121	1955	112	1996	117
1833	--	1874	129	1915	110	1956	127	1997	114
1834	--	1875	132	1916	122	1957	110	1998	103
1835	--	1876	132	1917	127	1958	114	1999	103
1836	--	1877	115	1918	116	1959	116	2000	100
1837	--	1878	108	1919	104	1960	115	2001	123
1838	--	1879	132	1920	120	1961	123	2002	102
1839	--	1880	111	1921	88	1962	116	2003	117
1840	--	1881	126	1922	96	1963	110	2004	109
1841	--	1882	119	1923	117	1964	119	2005	109
1842	--	1883	127	1924	110	1965	118	2006	93
1843	--	1884	123	1925	116	1966	116	2007	114
1844	--	1885	120	1926	124	1967	118	2008	114
1845	--	1886	114	1927	110	1968	105		
1846	--	1887	127	1928	121	1969	116		
1847	--	1888	135	1929	104	1970	121		

Table 25. Ice-out dates for Swan Lake, Maine.

[--, no data]

Location of lake—Latitude 44°32'47", longitude 68°59'38"

Period of record—1891 to 2008

Years of record—118

Observer—The Republican Journal, Duncan Brown

Year	Julian day	Year	Julian day	Year	Julian day	Year	Julian day	Year	Julian day
1807	--	1848	--	1889	--	1930	104	1971	121
1808	--	1849	--	1890	--	1931	103	1972	122
1809	--	1850	--	1891	109	1932	108	1973	106
1810	--	1851	--	1892	114	1933	108	1974	100
1811	--	1852	--	1893	124	1934	114	1975	116
1812	--	1853	--	1894	113	1935	116	1976	103
1813	--	1854	--	1895	112	1936	98	1977	109
1814	--	1855	--	1896	110	1937	106	1978	116
1815	--	1856	--	1897	115	1938	106	1979	95
1816	--	1857	--	1898	109	1939	127	1980	103
1817	--	1858	--	1899	117	1940	122	1981	88
1818	--	1859	--	1900	109	1941	108	1982	107
1819	--	1860	--	1901	112	1942	112	1983	97
1820	--	1861	--	1902	90	1943	114	1984	110
1821	--	1862	--	1903	92	1944	119	1985	97
1822	--	1863	--	1904	122	1945	93	1986	99
1823	--	1864	--	1905	110	1946	101	1987	106
1824	--	1865	--	1906	114	1947	102	1988	100
1825	--	1866	--	1907	120	1948	102	1989	110
1826	--	1867	--	1908	115	1949	99	1990	101
1827	--	1868	--	1909	108	1950	111	1991	99
1828	--	1869	--	1910	92	1951	96	1992	111
1829	--	1870	--	1911	120	1952	108	1993	114
1830	--	1871	--	1912	115	1953	86	1994	108
1831	--	1872	--	1913	99	1954	110	1995	104
1832	--	1873	--	1914	119	1955	106	1996	105
1833	--	1874	--	1915	101	1956	120	1997	113
1834	--	1875	--	1916	113	1957	104	1998	94
1835	--	1876	--	1917	118	1958	109	1999	89
1836	--	1877	--	1918	116	1959	112	2000	97
1837	--	1878	--	1919	98	1960	112	2001	124
1838	--	1879	--	1920	117	1961	123	2002	99
1839	--	1880	--	1921	88	1962	112	2003	117
1840	--	1881	--	1922	104	1963	112	2004	110
1841	--	1882	--	1923	119	1964	116	2005	107
1842	--	1883	--	1924	109	1965	111	2006	91
1843	--	1884	--	1925	94	1966	110	2007	109
1844	--	1885	--	1926	123	1967	121	2008	112
1845	--	1886	--	1927	107	1968	107		
1846	--	1887	--	1928	112	1969	115		
1847	--	1888	--	1929	111	1970	115		

Table 26. Ice-out dates for Thompson Lake, Maine.

[--, no data]

Location of lake—Latitude 44°03'58", longitude 70°29'07"

Period of record—1902 to 2008

Years of record—102

Observers—Joseph M. Trebilcook, Richard Greenleaf, Thompson Lake Environmental Association, *www.mainelakecharts.com*

Year	Julian day	Year	Julian day	Year	Julian day	Year	Julian day	Year	Julian day
1807	--	1848	--	1889	--	1930	114	1971	123
1808	--	1849	--	1890	--	1931	102	1972	127
1809	--	1850	--	1891	--	1932	112	1973	110
1810	--	1851	--	1892	--	1933	114	1974	106
1811	--	1852	--	1893	--	1934	113	1975	103
1812	--	1853	--	1894	--	1935	113	1976	107
1813	--	1854	--	1895	--	1936	104	1977	109
1814	--	1855	--	1896	--	1937	117	1978	121
1815	--	1856	--	1897	--	1938	107	1979	104
1816	--	1857	--	1898	--	1939	126	1980	103
1817	--	1858	--	1899	--	1940	128	1981	88
1818	--	1859	--	1900	--	1941	105	1982	118
1819	--	1860	--	1901	--	1942	108	1983	100
1820	--	1861	--	1902	107	1943	116	1984	112
1821	--	1862	--	1903	94	1944	120	1985	101
1822	--	1863	--	1904	121	1945	93	1986	102
1823	--	1864	--	1905	113	1946	96	1987	100
1824	--	1865	--	1906	113	1947	106	1988	102
1825	--	1866	--	1907	120	1948	100	1989	118
1826	--	1867	--	1908	116	1949	100	1990	105
1827	--	1868	--	1909	110	1950	114	1991	99
1828	--	1869	--	1910	95	1951	100	1992	101
1829	--	1870	--	1911	118	1952	111	1993	113
1830	--	1871	--	1912	94	1953	96	1994	114
1831	--	1872	--	1913	108	1954	110	1995	104
1832	--	1873	--	1914	113	1955	107	1996	106
1833	--	1874	--	1915	105	1956	123	1997	113
1834	--	1875	--	1916	110	1957	107	1998	99
1835	--	1876	--	1917	118	1958	109	1999	96
1836	--	1877	--	1918	114	1959	113	2000	99
1837	--	1878	--	1919	102	1960	116	2001	--
1838	--	1879	--	1920	116	1961	121	2002	--
1839	--	1880	--	1921	93	1962	113	2003	112
1840	--	1881	--	1922	107	1963	110	2004	--
1841	--	1882	--	1923	114	1964	118	2005	--
1842	--	1883	--	1924	110	1965	119	2006	--
1843	--	1884	--	1925	100	1966	112	2007	113
1844	--	1885	--	1926	123	1967	118	2008	114
1845	--	1886	--	1927	107	1968	107		
1846	--	1887	--	1928	112	1969	110		
1847	--	1888	--	1929	113	1970	118		

Table 27. Ice-out dates for Umbagog Lake, New Hampshire/Maine.

[--, no data]

Location of lake—Latitude 44°48'05", longitude 71°01'42"

Period of record—1880 to 2008

Years of record—118

Observers—Union Water Power Company, FPL Energy Maine

Year	Julian day	Year	Julian day	Year	Julian day	Year	Julian day	Year	Julian day
1807	--	1848	--	1889	119	1930	122	1971	129
1808	--	1849	--	1890	131	1931	111	1972	135
1809	--	1850	--	1891	--	1932	121	1973	117
1810	--	1851	--	1892	--	1933	125	1974	130
1811	--	1852	--	1893	141	1934	116	1975	129
1812	--	1853	--	1894	--	1935	125	1976	113
1813	--	1854	--	1895	--	1936	121	1977	118
1814	--	1855	--	1896	123	1937	129	1978	132
1815	--	1856	--	1897	--	1938	117	1979	117
1816	--	1857	--	1898	--	1939	131	1980	117
1817	--	1858	--	1899	128	1940	131	1981	111
1818	--	1859	--	1900	--	1941	109	1982	127
1819	--	1860	--	1901	119	1942	121	1983	122
1820	--	1861	--	1902	112	1943	131	1984	121
1821	--	1862	--	1903	106	1944	126	1985	121
1822	--	1863	--	1904	114	1945	103	1986	110
1823	--	1864	--	1905	119	1946	116	1987	108
1824	--	1865	--	1906	131	1947	128	1988	115
1825	--	1866	--	1907	131	1948	115	1989	126
1826	--	1867	--	1908	122	1949	112	1990	118
1827	--	1868	--	1909	134	1950	126	1991	118
1828	--	1869	--	1910	100	1951	118	1992	130
1829	--	1870	--	1911	126	1952	118	1993	121
1830	--	1871	--	1912	124	1953	114	1994	125
1831	--	1872	--	1913	120	1954	122	1995	116
1832	--	1873	--	1914	130	1955	114	1996	125
1833	--	1874	--	1915	116	1956	128	1997	123
1834	--	1875	--	1916	125	1957	115	1998	109
1835	--	1876	--	1917	130	1958	122	1999	119
1836	--	1877	--	1918	118	1959	117	2000	113
1837	--	1878	--	1919	121	1960	119	2001	123
1838	--	1879	--	1920	129	1961	130	2002	110
1839	--	1880	129	1921	100	1962	122	2003	121
1840	--	1881	135	1922	117	1963	119	2004	120
1841	--	1882	141	1923	123	1964	123	2005	116
1842	--	1883	134	1924	124	1965	124	2006	109
1843	--	1884	--	1925	116	1966	123	2007	123
1844	--	1885	--	1926	129	1967	122	2008	118
1845	--	1886	--	1927	110	1968	110		
1846	--	1887	--	1928	130	1969	126		
1847	--	1888	144	1929	121	1970	130		

Table 28. Ice-out dates for West Grand Lake, Maine.

[--, no data]

Location of lake—Latitude 45°12'56", longitude 67°48'52"

Period of record—1878 to 2008

Years of record—131

Observers—Marion Staples and family (three generations)

Year	Julian day	Year	Julian day	Year	Julian day	Year	Julian day	Year	Julian day
1807	--	1848	--	1889	116	1930	117	1971	123
1808	--	1849	--	1890	128	1931	111	1972	135
1809	--	1850	--	1891	124	1932	116	1973	117
1810	--	1851	--	1892	121	1933	119	1974	112
1811	--	1852	--	1893	129	1934	115	1975	124
1812	--	1853	--	1894	120	1935	125	1976	111
1813	--	1854	--	1895	122	1936	107	1977	122
1814	--	1855	--	1896	120	1937	119	1978	127
1815	--	1856	--	1897	124	1938	115	1979	113
1816	--	1857	--	1898	117	1939	131	1980	109
1817	--	1858	--	1899	117	1940	129	1981	100
1818	--	1859	--	1900	119	1941	117	1982	124
1819	--	1860	--	1901	115	1942	120	1983	104
1820	--	1861	--	1902	98	1943	121	1984	121
1821	--	1862	--	1903	110	1944	123	1985	113
1822	--	1863	--	1904	126	1945	103	1986	113
1823	--	1864	--	1905	118	1946	117	1987	112
1824	--	1865	--	1906	125	1947	114	1988	111
1825	--	1866	--	1907	125	1948	116	1989	126
1826	--	1867	--	1908	121	1949	106	1990	117
1827	--	1868	--	1909	126	1950	120	1991	118
1828	--	1869	--	1910	100	1951	103	1992	124
1829	--	1870	--	1911	123	1952	120	1993	117
1830	--	1871	--	1912	128	1953	98	1994	122
1831	--	1872	--	1913	110	1954	118	1995	118
1832	--	1873	--	1914	130	1955	115	1996	115
1833	--	1874	--	1915	110	1956	126	1997	118
1834	--	1875	--	1916	118	1957	119	1998	107
1835	--	1876	--	1917	124	1958	115	1999	97
1836	--	1877	--	1918	139	1959	124	2000	100
1837	--	1878	116	1919	119	1960	122	2001	125
1838	--	1879	130	1920	125	1961	132	2002	103
1839	--	1880	123	1921	100	1962	119	2003	126
1840	--	1881	123	1922	108	1963	124	2004	115
1841	--	1882	126	1923	126	1964	124	2005	114
1842	--	1883	129	1924	128	1965	122	2006	92
1843	--	1884	121	1925	104	1966	115	2007	121
1844	--	1885	125	1926	134	1967	125	2008	119
1845	--	1886	123	1927	113	1968	112		
1846	--	1887	131	1928	124	1969	124		
1847	--	1888	138	1929	120	1970	121		

Table 29. Ice-out dates for Lake Winnipesaukee, New Hampshire.

[--, no data]

Location of lake—Latitude 43°35'56", longitude 71°19'21"

Period of record—1887 to 2008

Years of record—122

Observers—New Hampshire Office of Vacation Travel, Harry Daniel, Arthur Marshall, Bob Aldrich, The Lakes Region Association, The Classic Journey Company, *www.winnipesaukee.com*

Comments—Ice-out definition for most years is thought to have been the earliest date of open navigation for the MS *Mount Washington* on its regular route, except for Meredith Bay.

Year	Julian day	Year	Julian day	Year	Julian day	Year	Julian day	Year	Julian day
1807	--	1848	--	1889	104	1930	97	1971	126
1808	--	1849	--	1890	114	1931	101	1972	123
1809	--	1850	--	1891	113	1932	111	1973	106
1810	--	1851	--	1892	102	1933	115	1974	106
1811	--	1852	--	1893	130	1934	111	1975	115
1812	--	1853	--	1894	110	1935	111	1976	107
1813	--	1854	--	1895	116	1936	99	1977	113
1814	--	1855	--	1896	114	1937	115	1978	117
1815	--	1856	--	1897	113	1938	107	1979	116
1816	--	1857	--	1898	104	1939	124	1980	108
1817	--	1858	--	1899	122	1940	125	1981	95
1818	--	1859	--	1900	116	1941	106	1982	119
1819	--	1860	--	1901	110	1942	108	1983	100
1820	--	1861	--	1902	94	1943	120	1984	111
1821	--	1862	--	1903	92	1944	124	1985	104
1822	--	1863	--	1904	120	1945	91	1986	106
1823	--	1864	--	1905	114	1946	89	1987	102
1824	--	1865	--	1906	116	1947	114	1988	107
1825	--	1866	--	1907	119	1948	101	1989	115
1826	--	1867	--	1908	112	1949	108	1990	112
1827	--	1868	--	1909	109	1950	110	1991	98
1828	--	1869	--	1910	96	1951	104	1992	112
1829	--	1870	--	1911	122	1952	111	1993	112
1830	--	1871	--	1912	114	1953	93	1994	113
1831	--	1872	--	1913	107	1954	106	1995	105
1832	--	1873	--	1914	105	1955	109	1996	108
1833	--	1874	--	1915	114	1956	126	1997	114
1834	--	1875	--	1916	107	1957	93	1998	97
1835	--	1876	--	1917	118	1958	103	1999	98
1836	--	1877	--	1918	114	1959	116	2000	101
1837	--	1878	--	1919	104	1960	110	2001	122
1838	--	1879	--	1920	115	1961	117	2002	95
1839	--	1880	--	1921	87	1962	114	2003	115
1840	--	1881	--	1922	107	1963	110	2004	111
1841	--	1882	--	1923	114	1964	119	2005	110
1842	--	1883	--	1924	109	1965	112	2006	93
1843	--	1884	--	1925	100	1966	110	2007	113
1844	--	1885	--	1926	122	1967	110	2008	114
1845	--	1886	--	1927	103	1968	106		
1846	--	1887	127	1928	110	1969	115		
1847	--	1888	133	1929	108	1970	118		

www.ingramcontent.com/pod-product-compliance
Lightning Source LLC
Chambersburg PA
CBHW080350290526
45791CB00009BA/2810